WEDDINGS UNTANGLED:
THE QUICK STARTER FOR PLANNING YOUR WEDDING WITHOUT BREAKING THE BANK

BROUGHT TO YOU BY WEDDINGS UNTANGLED, LLC

Shauna LeBlanc Vaughan
and
Sheila Allen LeBlanc

Cover Design: Jamie Miller (www.jamieinpixels.com)

Editor & Interior Book Design: Constance H. Marse, BMF Enterprises

Library of Congress Control Number: 2012918789

ISBN-13: 978-1480034297 (CreateSpace-Assigned)

ISBN-10: 1480034290

Printed in Charleston, S.C.

DEDICATION

"A wedding is a wonderful thing, but it's not any less wonderful when it doesn't cost an arm and a leg."

—Dave Ramsey

To the brides who agree.

ACKNOWLEDGMENTS

The hardest part of these acknowledgments was deciding where to begin! When we sat back and wrote down the names of the people who have lent support in one way or another to make this happen, we were amazed at the number of people. Wow, we owe thanks to so many people.

Inspiration

Thank you to Robin Linde and Carlo Adair. The two of you are a beacon of inspiration that helped fuel this project. Your friendship and positivity are uncommon, and we are grateful for it.

Shauna's friend Karrie Anderson also energized this project. Thank you, Karrie, for humoring Shauna and her ideas. This project was only a dream for Shauna, and what began as a conversation about pants wound up ultimately giving her the gusto to throw caution to the wind. The conversation about pants is only on hold — for now.

Big thanks to Karrie Moore who unknowingly inspired this project. Your entrepreneurship and what has been called a "pioneer woman" approach to life is refreshing.

In the trenches

This book would not be what it is without the talents of Constance Marse and Jamie Miller. Connie, thank you for your patience and attention to detail with copy edit, layout, and design. You went above and beyond, and we are grateful. Jamie, we are thankful that we found you only by chance. Shauna made the right phone call to the right person (on a whim) at the right time. We thank you for your insistence on quality and your willingness to "blue sky" with us. Thanks to you, we have an amazing cover design.

Support

We had the support of a small village comprised of friends and family who provided feedback, opinions, and advice throughout this journey. Thank you to our husbands, Dustin and Terry, who are supportive in ways we often never expect. Thank you, Allison LeBlanc for your reliability, support, advice, honesty, and for always being a sounding board. We are grateful to Jason LeBlanc for the late night chats about various and sundry things. I bet you didn't know it was so helpful to just "shoot the breeze" about our wild ideas. Thank you also to Thomas Gorence who, despite having his own major project, lent support via thought-partnership and commiseration. You have no idea how appreciative we are that Shauna could reach out to you as someone who is also working on a major project. We can't wait to get our copy!

Often, friends lent a hand and may not have realized just how helpful it was. There were several people who provided thoughts and feedback as we drafted copy, received, comps for art work, and had late night and early morning ideas. A big hug and a warm thank you to Joey Hannes, Miles Carr, Charles Moore, Zachary Anderson, Heather Reynolds, Yvette Ruiz, Oliver Manuel, and Justin LeBlanc. We are so grateful for your support and willingness to help. ♥

TABLE OF CONTENTS

ABOUT THE AUTHORS

Sheila and Shauna are a mother-daughter team who survived (yes, they will tell you *survived* is the appropriate word) the wedding planning process, which led them to this book project. Although "survived" seems like an awful word of choice for what many deem to be an exciting time of life, these two will tell you that wedding planning is not easy, and the excitement wears off after awhile. Their intent in writing this book is to provide brides-to-be (and perhaps their mothers and their fiancés) with a starting point for a planning process that should be fun and rewarding, but often turns into stressful headaches, arguments with your loved ones, and a needless financial burden.

When Shauna was growing up, she and Sheila both dreamed of her wedding day and envisioned it to be of epic, princess proportions. Then, not unlike many families early in the 21st century, they were faced with economic hardship. Shauna will tell you, in hindsight, that she learned a lot about what is most important to her and that she planned her wedding accordingly. Sheila will tell you she wasn't convinced that Shauna was making decisions based on what she really wanted, and instead was doing things differently than they had dreamed of only because finances wouldn't allow their dreams to become a reality. While Sheila was feeling guilty for not being able to make the wedding of epic, princess proportions a reality, Shauna was becoming more and more comfortable with doing something exactly opposite of that. Throughout her planning journey, she learned that she didn't want the princess wedding, which she began to refer to as a "circus production." She knew what she wanted and, more important, she knew what she wanted to spend, and ultimately, she refused to finance their wedding at the sake of their future.

Their advice is based on reflection on personal experiences, questions from newly engaged acquaintances, feedback and input from friends, and the desire to offer help to other brides and families or moms and daughters. They concluded that they do have strategies and advice to offer others who find themselves in a quandary as planning on a budget becomes overwhelming.

As a result, they are offering this guide that should provide some guidance or at least let other brides know that they are not alone in this process. ♥

INTRODUCTION
DREAMS VS. REALITY

So you're engaged! That dream has finally come true. The excitement is unparalleled. All of your friends congratulate you. The anticipation immediately heightens your awareness of all things wedding-related surrounding you. Enthusiasm is boundless and good wishes are all you hear. Then the questions start, of course — lots of them — like When? Where? Who? How? How many? How much? … What am I doing? Reality sets in…

Designed to help you quick start your wedding planning, this guide is intended to provide support as you determine what is required (must-haves), what you can live without (nice-to-haves), and what you absolutely do not want when it comes to your wedding. Included within these pages are a few exercises to assist you as you begin the wedding planning process. (Or perhaps you're in the thralls of planning and are so overwhelmed you don't know up from down and are seeking a way to prioritize your needs and must-haves from your nice-to-haves!) Consider having your fiancé also answer the questions within this guide so that you can plan together and create a special day that reflects both of your visions.

Let's explore your vision of your wedding with some thought-provoking questions. In an effort to relieve some stress, we suggest that you just get started—anywhere really. But we can provide some direction and logic in the planning process if you are willing to think, write a little, communicate when appropriate, and listen to your own thoughts as well as to your fiancé's to determine what it is you REALLY want to have on your special day. Gain a better perspective of what can become reality and what cannot — or should not. Then, turn your dreams into what might become a newly discovered reality. Good luck! ♥

CHAPTER ONE
PRE-ASSESSMENT

*I*n this chapter, you will put pen to paper and describe what you envision your wedding to be. In later chapters, we will fine-tune the ideas you describe in this chapter, and then we will begin to tailor your dreams to your budget. Let's get started!

Who?

Draft your guest list! At this point, do not consider any other factors like location, etc. Just make a list of EVERYONE you would invite as if the sky is the limit. You will review and revise the list numerous times, but you need to get started now. On another sheet of paper, in the pages provided in the back of this guide, or on your computer, go ahead and create your guest list. How many people do you plan to invite from your families? How many friends will you each invite? Who else are you planning to invite (i.e. coworkers, etc)? Be sure to include the names of those in your wedding party and all others who are hired (photographer, officiant, DJ, etc.)

When?

How soon do you plan to get married? Probably one of the most common mistakes is thinking that you have a long time to plan, especially if your potential date is a year or more away. Time passes quickly and sometimes does not promote luxury. Also, planning backward from your established wedding date may help you develop a personal timeline that will be helpful to you, rather than one that you may find online or in a planning binder found in stores. Go ahead and write down when you think you would like to get married. (Consider using the pages in the back of this guide.)

What?

What exactly *is* a wedding to you? Briefly describe your vision of a wedding below, on the pages in the back of this guide, or using another piece of paper if necessary. Think about what you daydreamed about and envisioned for a wedding before you became engaged. Your values, morals, upbringing, parental influences, and many other aspects, will be factors in determining what you want reflected in your wedding.

To me a wedding is ...

_____

_____

_____

_____

Where?

You described your wedding above, but dive deeper here with the actual setting of your wedding. Describe the background in your pictures. Whether it is a princess' castle, a beach at sunset, or an enchanted forest, this will be the big factor in determining where your ceremony and reception are to be held. Remember, the pictures will be moments in time captured for you to cherish forever. What does the scene look like in these pictures?

I envision my wedding taking place (where?) ...

_____

_____

_____

_____

How?

Describe your ceremony briefly below, in the pages provided in the back of this guide, or using another piece of paper. Often the ceremony is cut-and-dried or cookie-cutter, but more often now couples are choosing to customize their vows, modify ceremonies, or break traditions. Think about what you want and what is or will be meaningful to you as a couple. Your shared interests or common goals become extremely important, and they can influence a wedding day that is reflective of your personalities, backgrounds, or character.

_____

_____

_____

_____

How much?

What is you estimated budget for the wedding you described on the previous pages, or for the wedding of your dreams? As you plan, you will want to consider the financial component of the wedding and reception. Who pays — and for what — are huge questions in most wedding plans. If you are lucky enough not to have to worry about finances, then you probably would not be reading this guide; therefore, we are assuming that you, like us, are concerned about the costs of the many elements involved in planning and also need to make some decisions about what is really important. Jeopardizing your financial future may not be what you want to do at this time, and certainly, you do not have to do that. Think about what is important and lasting and about your future together. For our purposes, we have selected the following monetary guides to use in planning.

Before you move forward with the exercises that follow, please circle the monetary range below that you think most accurately reflects the wedding that you described in the preceding sections.

$0-$1K	$5-7K
$1-3K	$7-10K
$3-5K	$10K+

CHAPTER TWO
DRILLING DOWN

Next, we'll go through a few exercises to distinguish what are must-haves, nice-to-haves, and those things that you can absolutely do without on your wedding day. For the categories that follow (Who? What? Where? When? How Much?) you will find that we have listed some items as non-negotiable. Those are the things that must happen for any wedding to be official or legal.

Use the checkboxes to categorize each item listed. There is space to include any items, people, things, etc., that are not listed.

Who?

Non-negotiable: bride, groom, officiant, a minimum of two witnesses

Considerations for "Who"

If you've read other books or consulted other resources for cost-saving strategies for weddings and receptions, then you will find that the number one piece of advice for saving money is to **limit your guest list and/or wedding party.**

Revisit the guest list you created in the last chapter. Do you want to send invitations or announcements to all those on your guest list? Sending an invitation means that you would be okay with (or want or expect) all of those who receive them showing up to your wedding and reception. In other words, you expect an RSVP. Announcements sometimes are sent in lieu of invitations, and can be formatted a number of ways to politely explain that it's just an announcement, a family affair, or to avoid some situations that you may not want to address. You also could announce your elopement after the fact. If you plan to send announcements, keep a separate list of the people who will receive those.

As you are reviewing and revising your guest list, remember that you can invite friends without having to include them in a wedding party. Contrary to popular belief, bridal parties are NOT required! They create additional costs (i.e. gifts, transportation, makeup, hair, etc.) before, during, and after your wedding. Not to mention they can — plain and simple — cause DRAMA, which can be costly in other ways.

Destination weddings can help limit the number of people who RSVP (thereby saving you money) *because* it may cost invitees more money to get to your wedding. Remember it will also cost YOU in the form of travel, lodging, transportation, and meals. If you are considering a destination wedding, it is a good idea to check potential travel costs for those most important to have with you such as family or special friends. Will you be paying for the cost of travel and lodging for your guests? Will there be a cost involved in making travel arrangements?

It is up to you to determine what you want and WITH WHOM you want to share your wedding day experience. Simply put, more people in attendance equates to more expense. This is why you will want to keep separate lists of those who are invited and those who will only receive announcements of your nuptials.

Rethink Your Guest List! Typically, the first draft of the guest list is not the final version. In this exercise, you will rate the people on your guest list using the "must have," "nice-to-have," and "absolutely not" rankings. The next chart lists some of the most common invitees to weddings, and it provides a good first step for reviewing and revising your guest list. If your drafted guest list from chapter one includes more people than are on this chart, then — after you complete this chart — continue ranking the remaining people on your list according to these same criteria. Again, as with all of the exercises in this book, you and your fiancé should participate in this exercise as you discuss and plan your wedding.

	Must Have	Nice-to-have	Absolutely not!
Wedding party			
Maid of Honor			
Best Man			
Bridesmaids (How many?)			
Groomsmen (How many?)			
Flower Girl			
Ring Bearer			
Parental units			

Mom			
Dad			
Stepmom			
Stepdad			
Grandparents			
Extended family			
Friends			
Coworkers			
Musicians/DJ			
Photographer			
Wedding planner			
Others (List them below, on another sheet of paper (on the pages provided in the back of this guide), or consult the guest list you created earlier, as suggested above.)			

When?

Non-negotiable: You must take time to prepare, meet legal requirements, and fulfill any obligations or personal prerequisites — even if you are eloping. For example, some places require that you file for your marriage license within a specified time frame before your wedding. You should plan for that and check any other local or state requirements.

Considerations for "When"

You should know that some months in the year are considered "peak season" for weddings and that this varies regionally. The weather may be more pleasant at certain times of the year, or particular venues may be more popular or available during certain seasons — factors that can affect overall cost of the wedding.

The day of the week you choose could influence the cost of your wedding. Sundays usually cost less due to lack of popularity for weddings. Particular dates, or popular dates, often cost more because availability is limited (for instance Valentine's Day). You will want to check on this if you already have a day of the week (or a specific date) in mind.

Time of day can affect cost as well. Often, afternoons or brunches cost less depending on the place or primary function of the business. Some times of day cost less than others depending upon the fashionable or traditional times for a venue. Factors that are personal to you — such as travel, special requests or special times — may help determine what time of day you select.

Having only one date in mind can be too limiting and cause additional stress and more work, because you may have to call more venues and/ or vendors based on availability. Unless you're starting well in advance, seeking a popular date like Valentine's day or other holiday or a holiday weekend (for instance, 10/10/10 was popular when Shauna was planning) may mean calling around until you find a venue and/or particular vendor with availability. Narrowing in on a specific date, if not done well in advance, may cause you to have to sacrifice the ideal venue, photographer, etc. because they book up quickly, sometimes years in advance, for popular dates or times of day because unique locations and providers book up quickly.

Use the chart below to rank the options related to the "when" factor of your wedding that are important to you as you plan.

	Must Have	Nice-to-have	Absolutely not!
Season			
Spring			
Summer			
Fall			
Winter			
Month			
Choice #1			
Choice #2			
Choice #3			
Day of the week			
Monday			
Tuesday			
Wednesday			
Thursday			
Friday			
Saturday			
Sunday			
Time of Day (ceremony start time)			
Before noon			
Between noon and 3 pm			
Between 3 pm and 6 pm			
Between 6 pm and 9 pm			

Looking at your preferences in the chart above, narrow it down to the top three dates and times that you would like to consider and list them below.

#1 Date: _____ Time: _____

#2 Date: _____ Time: _____

#3 Date: _____ Time: _____

Make any notes that you need to this point:
(or on the pages provided in the back of this guide) ♥

_____

_____

_____

_____

_____

_____

_____

_____

_____

_____

_____

How?

Non-negotiable: Ensure the legality of your ceremony. (This can mean making sure your officiant is legal, and therefore your marriage is legal, or knowing state requirements and abiding by those rules.)

Considerations for "How"

Couples who decide to modify or abandon tradition potentially are faced with additional stressors. This can be further complicated if the families of the bride and groom have differing expectations, traditions, values, religions, demographics, cultures, etc.

If you are considering a destination wedding, you should examine and/or evaluate many other factors based on practicality and values. You even may have to prepare to justify or explain your desire to have a destination wedding — or the destination of choice — to friends and family. If you get hung up considering what everyone else wants, then you risk the wedding becoming less about you and the groom and more about pleasing everyone else. While compromise is often possible, do consider that this day should most reflect you and your fiancé's vision of your day.

If you are considering something less traditional (read: not what your parents might expect), then either prepare to stand by your decision or make concessions and compromises. Often, family and friends may expect you to maintain a more traditional approach. Good communication, as well as clearly expressed expectations, is important to ensure relationships endure after the event.

Use the chart below to rank the options related to the "how" factor of your wedding that are important to you as you plan.

	Must Have	**Nice-to-have**	**Absolutely not!**
Civil			
Religious			
Elope			
Customized/non-traditional			
Destination			
Military			

Where?

Non-negotiable: You must decide on a place, even if you elope.

Considerations for "Where"

"Where" is actually dependent on "how" and "when," and because these dependencies exist, you must determine which of the three is most important. This can be especially challenging when families are involved or differences are allowed to be a dominant factor. If a specific date "when" is required or preferred, then you may have to make concessions related to "where."

If the "how" is required, then "where" may be dictated by it: i.e. religious = how, then where = church, and vice versa. This certainly is a matter of choice but can create stress.

Use the chart below to rank the options related to the "where" factor of your wedding that are important to you as you plan.

	Must Have	Nice-to-have	Absolutely not!
Church or other religious center			
Specific region (of world or country)			
Specific state			
Specific city			
Specific venue			
Indoors			
Outdoors			
Special interest/ place of significance			

How Much?

Non-negotiable: You must have a monetary range ($0 to unlimited) — whether imposed by yourself or someone else. Yes, even if your budget IS unlimited … you must know that before you start to plan.

Considerations for "How much"

We have found that as a rule, wedding-related things cost more than you might think or more than the average just because it is for a wedding. Did you know there is a huge difference in cost for a corporate event versus a wedding at a hotel banquet center? Despite the fact that they are both events requiring banquet staff, food, and other resources, they often gouge the cost for an event if it is called a wedding. We don't make this stuff up! And we don't know why that happens, but it is true in our experience.

A meaningful or memorable event does not necessarily have to cost an excessive amount of money. And, the meaningful and lasting marriage is the factor that counts for years to come.

When calculating the cost of the food for your wedding, remember that you should factor in meals for all the vendors you hire, i.e. photographer, planner, DJ, caterers, etc., because it is expected that you will feed them. That's why you drafted your guest list as the very first exercise, and then you reviewed it in the "who" section! Go back to the list that you ranked according to "must have," "nice-to-have," and "absolutely not" and, now that you know how it will add to cost, re-evaluate who you really want to invite … and assume they will be there with bells on, awaiting free food and drinks!

Financing a wedding should be evaluated to determine the impact it may have on your financial future. It's just one day — and it isn't even a WHOLE day! And even if you have the cash, is it really worth breaking the bank for a four- or five-hour event? We would argue that it isn't, and that you should save that money for your "happily ever after."

For example, if you plan to buy a house, will the four-hour wedding event jeopardize those plans and your ability to do so? Or if your parents are forking out the money, whether cash or credit, are you jeopardizing *their* financial situation?

No matter the cost, your wedding marks a lifetime commitment and is designed to celebrate your vows. You do not need to impress anyone. Your love and commitment should make an impression — not the almighty dollar (or several thousands in some cases)! Contrary to popular belief, weddings are not a spectator sport and are not required to be lavish circus productions.

Use the chart below to rank the cost factor that you are sure of as you plan.

	Target	Less Likely	Absolutely not!
$0-1K			
$1K-3K			
$3K-5K			
$5K-7K			
$7K-10K			
$10K+			

Make any notes that you need to this point:
(or on the pages provided in the back of this guide)

_____

_____

_____

_____

_____

_____

_____

_____

REVIEW

Now that you have completed the exercises, you are ready to review and re-evaluate. By writing the answers to the following questions, you may be able to think more clearly about your own wishes and what is important for you (and your future spouse) on your wedding day. Take time to think and answer.

After going through the exercises in this book, what are your key learnings or ah-ha moments?

(What had you not thought of before or what surprised you?)

_____

_____

_____

_____

_____

What are you willing to eliminate now that you have gone through these exercises?

_____

_____

_____

_____

_____

What did you discover you can live without?

_____

_____

_____

_____

_____

_____

What are your top three must-haves?

_____

_____

_____

_____

_____

_____

CHAPTER THREE
MAKING YOUR DREAMS A REALITY

*A*t this point (after the exercises in the previous chapters), you may be frustrated. We feel your pain! You may have discovered that you will need to readjust your priorities and/or rethink your budget. Rest assured. This can be done without compromising your dream.

A wedding event has two major components: the ceremony and the reception. It is important to determine which is (more) important or which you may want to spend more of your money on to make your day special.

The Ceremony

The ceremony is technically, of course, the legal portion of your day. Certain things must happen to be wed. If you determine that you are only concerned with the legal aspect of the event, then you actually may have taken a step to simplify the process. Depending upon your age, your parents and family, your fiancé, etc., you may need to make necessary concessions to keep peace.

The glamorous "princess" wedding is much different from the intimate bride/groom witnesses/officiant ceremony but, the result is actually the same—both couples are legally married and hope to have a happily-ever-after future.

The factors that determine the lavish vs. the simple are as varied as the couples themselves. The bottom line is that you have to be happy with your ceremony and your decisions that are involved with it. It is, after all, your day.

The Reception

The reception also can take on many faces depending upon your wishes, your budget, and your planning. This component of the wedding event can be extremely expensive. Again, the event should reflect your preferences and will depend largely upon what you can afford. There are literally hundreds of venues from which to choose with hundreds of varieties of food, beverage, and entertainment options. The many options can be overwhelming and packages can seem inflexible, potentially causing you to consider exceeding your budget.

The components of the reception usually include food, drink, dancing or entertainment, wedding cake, certain ceremonies or traditions, etc. Receptions are as varied as the couples who are married. Is your intent to have a party, entertain your guests, visit all of your guests, have time to spend with your guests, take a million photos?

Think of the wedding you envisioned in the first chapter of the guide —

when you wrote down your initial thoughts. Using the table below, go ahead and rank the various components of your wedding.

	Must Have	Nice-to-have	Absolutely not!
Attire & Accessories			
Wedding gown			
Alterations			
Veil and accessories			
Tuxedo (rent or purchase)			
Beauty (include cost of bridal party, if applicable)			
Hair			
Makeup			
Nails			
Entertainment			
Music (DJ, live band, etc.)			
Other?			
Flowers & Décor			
Bridal bouquet			
Bridal party bouquets			
Boutonnieres & corsages			
Ceremony décor			
Reception décor (including centerpieces, flowers, linens, etc.)			
Invitations & Stationery			
Engagement announcements & save the dates			
Invitations			

Postage (for all of the above, including RSVP cards)			
Reception menus			
Ceremony programs			
Guest book			
Place cards			
Thank you cards (sometimes included as a package with invites)			
Gifts & Favors			
Attendant gifts			
Parent gifts			
Gratuities for all service providers			
Wedding favors			
Jewelry			
Wedding bands			
Photography & Video			
Engagement session			
Photographer			
Videographer			
Digital cd/dvd of pictures			
Prints			
Album			
Planner Options			
Day-of coordinator			
Full service			
À-la-carte services			
Transportation			
Limo rental			

Other transportation (airfare, etc.)			
Rental Fees			
Ceremony location/site fees			
Officiator			
Reception location site/rental fee (tent, etc.)			
Linens, flatware, tableware, etc.)			
Hotel accommodations			
Other costs?			
Food and Drink			
Reception food			
Reception cake			
Reception drinks/bar			
Rehearsal dinner			
Miscellaneous			

NOTES

♥

CHAPTER FOUR
THE ZERO-BASED BRIDAL BUDGET™

*I*magine that you have $5000 to plan your wedding, and not a penny more. To some this will seem like too little, and to others $5K is more than they can afford. If $5K is more than your intended budget, then take your intended budget and cut it in half. Work with that amount for this exercise. The goal is spend every penny of the $5000. You do NOT have to plan to spend money on all of the items listed (you may not desire some items, so you should skip them), but you must spend all of your money. The objective here is to help you gain a better idea of what is truly most important to you — and considering the bottom line often helps brides to do just that!

	Budget	Amount remaining
BALANCE: $5000.00		
Attire & Accessories		
Wedding gown		
Alterations		
Veil and accessories		
Tuxedo (rent or purchase)		
Beauty (include cost of bridal party, if applicable)		
Hair		
Makeup		
Nails		
Entertainment		
Music (DJ, live band, etc.)		
Other?		
Flowers & Decor		
Bridal bouquet		
Bridal party bouquets		
Boutonnieres & corsages		
Ceremony décor		
Reception décor (including centerpieces, flowers, linens, etc.)		
Invitations & Stationery		
Engagement announcements & save the dates		
Invitations		
Postage (for all of the above, including RSVP cards)		
Reception menus		

Ceremony programs		
Guest book		
Place cards		
Thank you cards (sometimes included as a package with invites)		
Gifts & Favors		
Attendant gifts		
Parent gifts		
Gratuities for all service providers		
Wedding favors		
Jewelry		
Wedding bands		
Photography & Video		
Engagement session		
Photographer		
Videographer		
Digital cd/dvd of pictures		
Prints		
Album		
Planner Options		
Day-of coordinator		
Full service		
À-la-carte services		
Transportation		
Limo rental		
Other transportation (airfare, etc.)		
Rental Fees		
Ceremony location/site fees		

Officiator		
Reception location site/rental fee (tent, etc.)		
Linens, flatware, tableware, etc.)		
Hotel accommodations		
Other costs?		
Food and Drink		
Reception food		
Reception cake		
Reception drinks/bar		
Rehearsal dinner		
Miscellaneous		

CHAPTER FIVE
BACK TO THE FUTURE

Happy Anniversary!

Imagine it is now *one year from your wedding day.*
What would you like to be remembering about your day? Be specific!

_____

_____

_____

Now imagine it is *five years from your wedding day.*
What do you hope to remember about your wedding day on this anniversary?

_____

_____

_____

NOTES

♥

FINAL THOUGHTS

Chances are, you picked up this book with hopes that it would help you with your planning in some way (likely to help gain some perspective on what you can afford). Our objective is to assist the bride who is searching for an affordable wedding. Ultimately, we aim to make lavish, expensive weddings a thing of the past by inspiring brides (and their family members) to avoid making them into "circus productions," as Shauna says.

Remember that this book can be used as a guide, even after you have finished the exercise. When you're stressed about something planning-related or are losing sight of what you wrote in these pages, go back to the exercises that you completed through the pages of this book that list your preferences. Use them as a reminder of what is most important to you and your fiancé. Remember that weddings do not have to be cookie-cutter, and that you can (and should) think outside the box to avoid financing your future or breaking the bank.

Best wishes to you as you begin, continue and/or complete your own wedding event. Remember this is one day in your life — the days that remain are equally important to you as a married couple as you live happily ever after—that was your goal, right? Remember — **keep things in perspective. And don't break the bank! ♥**

NOTES

♥

NOTES

♥

NOTES

_____

_____

_____

_____

_____

_____

_____

_____

_____

_____

_____

_____

_____

_____

_____

♥

NOTES

NOTES

_____

_____

_____

_____

_____

_____

_____

_____

_____

_____

_____

_____

_____

_____

_____

_____

♥

NOTES

♥